There Are Millions of Churches

Why Is the World Going to Hell?

Bill Vincent

Litchfield, IL 62056

© 2014 by Bill Vincent.

All rights reserved. No part of this book may be reproduced, stored in a retrieval system or transmitted in any form or by any means without the prior written permission of the publishers, except by a reviewer who may quote brief passages in a review to be printed in a newspaper, magazine or journal.

First Printing

Revival Waves of Glory Books & Publishing has allowed this work to remain exactly as the author intended, verbatim, without editorial input.

All Scripture quotations are from the Authorized King James Version of the Bible unless otherwise noted.

Ebook 978-1-304-97875-2

Softcover 978-1-304-97872-1

Hardcover 978-1-304-97874-5

PUBLISHED BY REVIVAL WAVES OF GLORY BOOKS & PUBLISHING

www.revivalwavesofgloryministries.com

Litchfield, IL

Printed in the United States of America

Table of Contents

Introduction 5

Chapter One Facts and Figures 7

Chapter Two Worshipping the Stars Rather Than God 11

Chapter Three Divisions and Doctrines 15

Chapter Four Why Are There So Many Churches? 19

Chapter Five WHY THE WORLD IS GOING TO HELL 29

Chapter Six What the Hell 33

Chapter Seven Going to Hell 41

Chapter Eight The Dead Church 45

About the Author 55

Recommended Books 57

Introduction

Whether everyone will admit it or not, the traditional church is in deep trouble and has been struggling for years to survive. There is a small rise of some new, non-traditional churches that help us all realize that God truly has a new way of doing Church. There is no easy fixes but at the same time, there are real roots that are being revealed in this book. The Church does not need another program nor does it need another religious organization. We don't need religious leaders but compassionate, Christ centered leaders. Bill is a prophet of God with a strong Word that all of the Church needs to hear. Bill reveals that there are so many Churches both big and small meeting and keeping silent while the World gets worse in many areas. The fact of the matter is the world and even some Churches are on the road to Hell. We must hear the urgency of all that God has laid on the heart of Bill Vincent and many prophetic voices like him.

So many Churches in America why is America in such bad shape somebody is dropping the ball This why we can't just go to Church as spectators when we're asked to pray for a person or Country we need to take it seriously and really travail and intercede instead of shrugging it off and leaving it to the next person. This would be where someone would drop the ball. You know why bad things have happened in America because God is trying to wake this Country up and believe there is a higher power in this Country and it is not the President of the United States.

Chapter One

Facts and Figures

We are to start all of this with the numbers. It really reveals a real foundation to what this book will reveal. Currently there are over 3.7 million Christian congregations in the world. However, it is difficult to say the exact number of denomination because new denomination are formed daily, but it is believed that there are around 67,000 denominations with close to 50,000 new congregations being added each year. Most of this growth is in South America, Africa and Asia.

It is very hard to estimate the number of churches in the world. This is because millions of churches are mushrooming from left, right and center in many parts of the world especially in Africa and the Caribbean. People have commercialized the Christian faith to the extent that they only begin churches as a business venture.

Why are there so many denominations in the world when Jesus said that He would build His church? Why are there so many churches with so many different doctrines? Didn't Jesus say that He would build His one true church? Is there such a thing as the worldwide church?

There are an estimated 37 million churches in the world with 50,000 new ones added every year and no two are the same. There are so many churches because there are so many Christians in the world. In fact, one third of the world's population are Christ followers and it is growing exponentially too. These figures do not count the millions of underground and house churches where it is dangerous to profess your faith publicly. One lady in a Muslim country was thrashed and beaten for simply wearing a cross to school and the local police failed to file any charges against the school and in fact, threatened the lady herself that they could not possibly protect her if she ever wore a cross in public again. The school ripped the cross off of her neck and threw it in the trash.

The church is not actually a building but is composed of a body of believers, called the Body of Christ. This is why even house churches with just a few Christians can be considered a church by definition. Jesus said in Matthew 16:18 that *"I will build my church, and the gates of Hades will not overcome it."* The Greek word used for church is "ekklesia." The word "ekklesia" is found in one hundred and fifteen places in the New Testament. It is translated in English one hundred and thirteen times as "church" and the remaining times it is translated as an "assembly." In classical Greek the word "ekklesia" meant "an assembly of citizens summoned" which is a great definition. The "citizens" in this case are citizens of the Kingdom of Heaven...or the Body of Christ. Since Jesus said that the gates of Hades (literally, hell) will not prevail or stop His church from being built and the church will prevail even till the time of Christ's Second return, we know that the church will not be stopped by anything or anyone.

The writer of Hebrews constrains us to not be *"forsaking the assembling of ourselves together, as is the manner of some, but exhorting one another, and so much more as you see the Day approaching"* (Hebrews 10:25). If we should forsake the assembling of ourselves together, then it would be impossible to *"consider one another in order to stir up love and good works"* if we are being a lone ranger Christian. I've seen so many lone ranger ministries disconnect from and assembling together. In the New Testament churches, there are no lone ranger Christians and the epistles (letters) in the New Testament are written to specific churches at specific locations and were naturally written to the church members in them. Well over half of the New Testament contain these letters that are written to the churches and the Christians who attend them.

There are an estimated 34,000 plus denominations of churches in the world today including 1,200 in the U.S. alone. Why are there so many different denominations? What are the reasons behind this number of denominations when Jesus said that He would build His church, assuming it would be one, universal church (Matt 16:18)? Are all of these thousands of churches under the Headship of Christ Jesus? Most certainly not all of the churches nor all of the thousands of denominations teach sound biblical doctrine. Some are heretical and others teach a smorgasbord of beliefs from the Bible and other religions. Yet others teach that Jesus became God and was not God at one time. Some believe that even God the Father was at one time not a god. This teaching is contrary to what the Bible says (John 1).

Even though there are thousands of denominations, there really is no single church that has all known truth and teaches it perfectly. I know that as God has revealed more and more to me that I have found brand new truths in God's Word. I'm talking about things like I was taught "Lord if it be your will I will be healed". I discovered that it is always God's will to be healed. There is no one church that has absolutely no error, just like every Christian alive cannot possibly know all truth. As long as the essentials to the faith are there, like the Chief Cornerstone Jesus Christ being the central focus of worship, churches can still be under the Headship of Christ Jesus. If you look at nature, if you look at the human race, and if you look at the intricacies of human understanding, you see that God loves variety so it should not surprise us that there are a variety of different denominations embedded within different nations and cultures. I believe God loves such variety as long as there are no blatant doctrinal errors within the body of that church. God seeks the worship of all nations, all ethnic groups, all people groups, from all over the world.

Chapter Two
Worshipping the Stars Rather Than God

Whether you realize it or not we were designed to worship God with all of our heart, mind and soul. I have personally been introduced to a level of worship that actually moves God. I have not always found this but I know that the world is partially in the shape that it is in, because we have lost our worship. If you attend most local Churches in the world you will find a dead worship or a concert. Very few are worshipping God in Spirit and in truth. Before you disagree let's take a look at the Church when it comes to entertainment.

The United States and all over the world hit a new high during sporting events but when it is for the championship it becomes so commercialized in the world and even in the Church. First don't get me wrong I love to play sports and used to never miss a game. The thing is the closer I got to God the less important sports became. The Super Bowl – World Series has been introduced to even entertain the Church. Since when does the Church need another event that has no God in it. When we have sunk to a level of allowing a sport to infiltrate the Church, you can expect some serious consequences. I have personally witnessed Church members sitting around eating and drinking beer in the place of worship watching the Super Bowl. The world is going to hell, darkness is covering the Earth, and we allow our focus on sporting events. When our team gets a touchdown or a homerun we cheer and scream. On any given Sunday our worship is mundane. We cheer only if it is entertaining. If real worship can be rediscovered we will see the beginning of change and moving the Church in the right direction. A minister once referred to the

Super Bowl as men covered in plastic crashing into each other and fighting over some cowhide. I say all this because we have entered into a entertainment Church rather than a seeking God Church.

Have you ever looked at a Church member in a Concert? Then that same Christian in the local Church. It is the difference of night and day. We shout for one more song but are quiet on Sunday morning. I know you might say that your Church is on fire. I really hope that is true, but it is rare to see the hunger and desperation for God.

When we go to the movies, it may have been so funny or dramatic that we will talk about it for days. I say this because, when was the last time you were talking about Sunday Worship for days. Is God not showing up so much that you are impacted. I'm telling you we should have so much fun and be impacted every Sunday that we could talk about it for years. The only reason we wouldn't talk about everything is because we are continually impacted every Sunday and the rest of the week at home.

Another thing that can become a form of worship is the famous gossip magazines. Everyone loves to find out who is with who and some people buy these magazines when some Hollywood so and so is in it. Even if it is lies we have to read about it. When was the last time we had that kind of passion to read about Elijah, Moses or even Jesus.

All these things have infiltrated the Church because we have given place to them. Our prayer meetings our dead and our worship isn't turning God's head. Something has been happening to the Church for decades and it's called entertainment. We have colored lights and smoke machines. We have introductions of speakers like they are Gods. It has become a show to keep the attention of people saved or unsaved. There is a lack of fear of the Lord and worship. We don't see it until God reveals it. We don't need another flesh pleasing outreach or program. We need to come together and pray until Jesus comes.

Chapter Three
Divisions and Doctrines

These two things run hand in hand and where the new beliefs begin. Any church that does not teach the theology of Jesus Christ, that He was God before the earth existed, that there is a Holy Trinity, that Christ came to earth and was born of a virgin, lived a sinless, perfect life, and died to have the wrath of God placed on Him instead should have been placed on humans, that He was raised or resurrected on the third day and today sits at the right hand of God in Heaven, is not the one that Jesus Christ built and founded. It is simple as that.

I have been in Churches where the teaching has got so far off and the Church still says Amen. Any church that deviates from these essential and vital doctrines cannot be, based upon the written Word of God, the true church that Jesus founded and it is teaching a false gospel. If any of these basics are missing, take heed to God's warning through Paul's letter to the Galatians, *"As we have already said, so now I say again: If anybody is preaching to you a gospel other than what you accepted, let them be under God's curse"* (Galatians 1:9)! How much stronger of a warning can Paul be issuing to those churches or Christians who teach another gospel? They are "under God's curse."

"If anyone teaches otherwise and does not agree to the sound instruction of our Lord Jesus Christ and to godly teaching, they are conceited and understand nothing. They have an unhealthy

interest in controversies and quarrels about words that result in envy, strife, malicious talk, evil suspicions" (1 Timothy 6:3-4).

Some churches have actually divided over the color of carpet in the sanctuary. Others have divided over doctrine. What unites, or at least *should* unite churches and Christians, are the fundamentals of the faith. That is Jesus was with God in the beginning, came to be born as a human by a virgin birth, lived a sinless life, died on Calvary for our sins as the atonement, was resurrected on the third day, and ascended to heaven. If *any* of these essentials are not taught in a church, it is not the church that Christ built. THESE ARE NON-NEGOTIABLE. THESE TRUTHS CANNOT BE COMPROMISED. If they are compromised, then this is not Jesus' church...it is a false church teaching false doctrines. Having a majority of truth mixed with a tiny bit of heresy is a dangerous church and makes it like a cult. There are no shortages of churches that teach false gospels. Even in Paul's day many were *"turning to a different gospel — which is really no gospel at all. Evidently some people are throwing you into confusion and are trying to pervert the gospel of Christ"* (Galaltions 1:6b-7). Paul is saying that it is the FULL GOSPEL or it is *"NO GOSPEL AT ALL."*

There are so many debates between denominations today that it must surely grieve Jesus' heart. Many Christians and many churches take non-essentials and make heated debate over them. Others find no unity in the basics. And frequently both groups show no love toward one another. Since the non-essentials are not intended to create division and are not essential to salvation, why have these issues resulted in Christians attacking other Christians? Some believe in tongues and signs and wonders, some do not, some believe in foot washing, some do not and since these are non-essentials to salvation, they should not be causing such bitter strife, division, debate or even heated arguments. Where is the love that is Paul's focus on non-essentials in these cases?

Why not give grace to others who may not have exactly the same beliefs as you do in the non-essentials? Each Christian is different, each one has been raised with different views. Having differing views on non-essentials is no reason to engage in heated exchanges that end up in arguments. Imagine what Jesus would think if He saw and heard us quarreling over something that is not a foundational belief in our salvation? How mortified would Christ be, when churches divide over the color of the carpet? Even Jesus, when He had railing false accusations made against Him and outright boldface lies told about Him remained silent. Let us remember that *"When they hurled their insults at him, he did not retaliate; when he suffered, he made no threats. Instead, he entrusted himself to him who judges justly"* (1 Peter 2:23). In other words, would it not be better to suffer insult, attacks, or ridicule than to respond in kind?

If Paul and certainly Christ could hear all of the backbiting between Christians and between denominations today, they would both say to us, *"If I speak in the tongues of men or of angels, but do not have love, I am only a resounding gong or a clanging cymbal. If I have the gift of prophecy and can fathom all mysteries and all knowledge, and if I have a faith that can move mountains, but do not have love, I am nothing. If I give all I possess to the poor and give over my body to hardship that I may boast, but do not have love, I gain nothing. Love is patient, love is kind. It does not envy, it does not boast, it is not proud. It does not dishonor others, it is not self-seeking, it is not easily angered, it keeps no record of wrongs. Love does not delight in evil but rejoices with the truth. It always protects, always trusts, always hopes, always perseveres. Love never fails"* (1 Corinthians 13:1-8b). Repeating some important words here: love is kind, love is patient, it does not boast, it is not proud, it does not dishonor, it is not easily angered…love never fails. Let it be so among us in the non-essentials.

Church is considered the assembly of believers (though they meet in all parts of the world, at different times, in different buildings). Many churches are needed to support the third of the world's known population of Christians (and the underground population that must hide for safety).

Denominations are a man-made thing. Not all denominations, or even churches are under the Headship of Christ Jesus because some have drifted away from what the Bible teaches as essential doctrines. When a church deviates from the truth that is in the Bible, they are not part of the true Church. When they teach anything other than the true gospel, they should beware because the Bible warns against this (Galatians 1:9; 1 Timothy 6:3-4).

If you are interested in joining with a church, be sure to ask to see their statement of faith — if it does not line up with what the Bible teaches or if there is no statement of faith, think again and continue searching for a doctrinally sound church. Remember there is no perfect church because we as humans are not perfect, but Jesus taught us about the true Church and this is all recorded in the Bible. As Christians, we should have a biblical worldview and the only way to do that is to read the Bible to learn what it says about the subject at hand. STOP TAKING MINISTERS WORD FOR IT.

Chapter Four

Why Are There So Many Churches?

It is amazing how Churches begin with a new truth and then someone leaves and starts another truth. There being so many churches, how can we know what's right? I've been a member of a number of churches in my lifetime. Some big and some small. You name it. They all believe in the same God, but worship in a lot of different ways. Does it really matter?

Have you ever wondered why there are so many different churches and practices and beliefs? Is it possible that every denomination is right? Does God approve of this kind of division and confusion? And does it even really matter? Why are there so many different churches? Does it matter to God? Is He pleased with the current situation in the religious world?

If I were to ask you exactly how many different churches exist in the world today... what would you say? You would probably say, "I don't know...A lot I guess." And that would be right. There are a lot! You saw the numbers in the first Chapter.

I want you to think about how confusing this can be for a person who is seeking the truth. Because you have one church over here that is teaching this practice and another church that is teaching the opposite. One church says that item A is sinful and another church says that item A is mandatory. Who is right? Can they both be right?

Some people will tell you, "That is good!" "It is good to have variety." "Just attend the church of your choice." And they will say, "One church is just as good as another." "We are all going to the same place anyway." "There are just different paths leading us to the same location."

God is not the author of confusion.

When I read my New Testament, I read about only one church. But when I look around me today, and I see those who profess Christianity, I see thousands. Now the question is how did we get from one to thousands? And the answer is... something went wrong.

Something went severely wrong. But you see, It didn't go wrong with God. It went wrong with man.

Acts 2:47 says "The Lord added to the church daily those who were being saved." And this fits perfectly with what Jesus promised in Matthew 16:18. He promised A...upon this rock I will build My church."

The apostle Paul echoes the sentiment of the one church as he is speaking to the elders in Ephesus. He tells them to "Shepherd the church of God which He purchased with His own blood." (Acts 20:28)

In the book of Ephesians we are told that God has put all things under Christ's feet and gave Him to be the head over all things to the church which is His body..." And so the church of Christ and the body of Christ are the same thing. And then the singularity of the church is nailed down in Ephesians 4:4 when He says "There is one body."

I ask the question, how many Churches were there in the New Testament? One single Church. Well, what if someone came along and wanted to start some different divisions of that one church? Different denominations if you will. Would that be okay? And the answer to that question is, no. That would not be okay.

I want you to listen to the words of the apostle Paul as he writes to the church in Corinth.

"Now I plead with you brethren by the name of our Lord Jesus Christ that you all speak the same thing, and that there be no divisions among you, but that you be perfectly joined together in the same mind and the same judgment." I Corinthians 1:10

How does that network with what we see in the religious world today? With all of the different denominations and divisions and sects that are all teaching different things? And the answer is... It does not even come close at all. It is completely foreign to the New Testament concept of the church.

Now, more specifically, what was the problem with the church in Corinth? I want you to listen again.

This is verse twelve. Paul says "Now I say this, that each of you says, 'I am of Paul,' or 'I am of Apollos,' or 'I am of Cephas,' or 'I am of Christ.' Is Christ divided? Was Paul crucified for you? Or were you baptized in the name of Paul?"

You see, within the First Century Church, we see the seeds of denominationalism. Some were starting to hold to Paul, while others were holding to Apollos others to Cephas, to Peter, and others to Christ. Divisions were starting to form and Paul, by the inspiration of the Holy Spirit, condemns this. And he makes it clear that this is not of God.

Okay, as we seek to answer the question, "Why are there so many churches," I want us to notice that God predicted that there would be a departure from the New Testament pattern. You see, despite the clarity of the New Testament with regard to the oneness of the church and despite the warnings against division, God knew that divisions would come. In fact, the Bible foretells of it and warns against it several times.

One of these warnings comes from a passage we mentioned a moment ago. It's the conversation between Paul and the

Ephesian elders. He tells them to "shepherd the church..." which was purchased by the blood of Christ. He says that For I know this, that after my departure savage wolves will come in among you, not sparing the flock. Also from among yourselves men will rise up, speaking perverse things, to draw away the disciples after themselves."

Now, it is interesting that Paul tells the leaders of this church of this congregation that a departure would come from them. In addition, the reason that this is so interesting is because one of the first departures in the church was with regard to its leadership and its organization.

Now, another warning concerning departure is found in I Timothy, chapter 4. Let's read this one together.

It says, "Now the Spirit speaks expressly (that is the Holy Spirit is speaking very plainly here) that in the latter times some will depart from the faith, giving heed to seducing spirits and doctrines of demons, speaking lies and hypocrisy, having their own conscience seared with a hot iron, forbidding to marry, and commanding to abstain from foods which God created to be received with thanksgiving by those who believe and know the truth."

We will see in history that two of the specific departures that will later take place relate to forbidding marriage and not being allowed to eat certain foods. I'm talking about the Last Days.

Now, thus far we see that according to the New Testament pattern, there was only one church, but we also see that God predicted that there would be a departure from that New Testament pattern.

Alright, let's get to the key question. Why are there so many churches today? How did a basic Bible belief system with a unified group of people turn into literally thousands of different denominations with different practices and different beliefs?

Well, history tells us that very early on there came along splinter groups who had ideas and doctrines contrary to that of the first century church and contrary to the doctrine that they had received and practiced.

Hopefully now, you can see why there are so many churches. And here is the message that we really need to take to heart. Since Jesus condemns division, we need to be a part of that one church that Jesus established. The one that He bought with His blood. Not one of the manmade churches that came along later in history.

Now, what does all this mean for us today? Does this mean that denominations are wrong?

We want to be clear. And the answer is... **yes**, it would have to mean that. All churches other than the one built by Jesus Christ exist without New Testament authority or example.

Now somebody says, "Does that mean that good intentioned morally upright people in denominations will be lost?" Well, let's let the Lord answer this question.

I want you to hear the words of Jesus in Matthew 7:21 23, "Not everyone who says to me, 'Lord, Lord,' shall enter the kingdom of heaven but he who does the will of My Father in heaven. Many will say unto me in that day, 'Lord, Lord, have we not prophesied in Your name, cast out demons in Your name, and done many wonders in Your name?' And I will declare to them, never knew you; depart from Me, you who practice lawlessness!"

Jesus says that on the Day of Judgment there will be good people, people who are teachers, people who claim to hold to the name of Jesus, people who will be lost because they haven't done the will of the Father.

Now, the point is, having good intentions is not enough. Having my heart right is not enough. I actually have to follow the New Testament pattern.

Acts 2:47 A...praising God and having favor with all the people. The Lord added to the church daily those who were being saved.

All of the saved people are in the church. That one built by Jesus. The same one that existed in Acts chapter two. The same one that we read about throughout the New Testament. The one that existed prior to all the denominations of man.

Now, the question is "How do I become a part of that church? The one wherein is salvation. How do I become a part of the one church of the New Testament?" And the answer is... the same way they did it in the New Testament.

You've got to obey the Gospel.

You know sometimes people in the religious world will tell you that "There is nothing you have to obey." They will say that "You only need to believe." But I want you to listen to the words of Second Thessalonians, chapter 1, verses 7 and 8. The Bible says, "and to give you who are troubled rest with us when the Lord Jesus is revealed from heaven with his mighty angels,"

Now listen to this He is describing the day of judgment. He says that some people are going to receive rest, some people are going to receive punishment. He says "when the Lord comes in flaming fire taking vengeance on those who do not know God." Now listen. "...and on those who do not obey the gospel of our Lord Jesus Christ."

Your see, we must obey the gospel. Now, obeying the gospel can be summed up in five short words:

- ➢ Hear
- ➢ Believe
- ➢ Repent
- ➢ Confess
- ➢ and Baptism

Now, somebody says "What does that mean, explain that."

Well first, a man must hear the gospel. He hears that because of his sin he has transgressed the will of God and is destined to die eternally in Hell. (Romans 6:23) "The wages of sin is death." He also hears that Jesus Christ came as God in the flesh to pay the penalty for his sin so that he does not have to. He hears that, salvation is found in Christ. Romans 10:14 indicates if a person does not hear the message of the Gospel he has no hope.

Now, upon hearing it he must also believe it. Now what does that entail? What must a man believe? He must believe. He must understand that Jesus is the Christ the son of God. John 8:24 Jesus said, "If you believe not that I am He, you shall die in your sins." He must understand that Jesus is deity. (John 1:14) "And the Word was made flesh and dwelt among us, and we beheld His glory, the glory as of the only begotten of the Father, full of grace and truth." He must of course believe in the death, burial and resurrection of Christ. How it is that "while we were yet sinners, Christ died for us." (Romans 5:8) "Then he arose, defeating death." (1 Corinthians 15:54 55)

Romans 10:9 says, "that if you confess with your mouth the Lord Jesus Christ and believe in your heart that God has raised him from the dead, you will be saved." Of course, it is crucial that a man believe and understand the body of Christ which is the church of the New Testament. 2nd Timothy, 2:10, says, "salvation is in Christ."

Then a man must repent. Acts, chapter 17, verse 30, says, "Truly these times of ignorance God overlooked, but now commands all men everywhere to repent." Repentance is a change of mind brought about by Godly sorrow that results in a reformation of life. That is important to understand. Sometimes people will say, "Repentance is merely changing your life." That is not a good definition of repentance. Repentance is changing your mind. Of course, that is followed by a change of life.

A person must confess his faith in Christ. Romans 10, verse 10, clearly tells us, "For with the heart one believes unto righteousness, and with the mouth confession is made unto salvation." In Acts, chapter 8, as Philip was teaching the gospel to the Ethiopian, he said, "See here is water. What hinders me from being baptized?" Philip responded to the Ethiopian and said, "If you believe with all of your heart, you may." And he answered and said, "I believe Jesus Christ is the Son of God." That is the confession we are talking about. Not a confession of our sin. A confession of what we have heard and what we believe. It is an acknowledgment. "Yes, we believe these things."

Now finally, involved in obeying the gospel, one must be baptized. In Mark 16, verse 16, Jesus said, "He who believes and is baptized will be saved; but he who does not believe will be condemned." You know, baptism as practiced by First Century Christians was total immersion.

In fact that is the meaning of baptism. It is the point at which a person is immersed in water and the point at which he contacts the saving blood of Jesus. It is the point at which he has finally obeyed the gospel. Romans 6:3 and 4 says, "Or do you not know that as many of us as were baptized into Christ Jesus were baptized into His death? Therefore we were buried with Him through baptism into death, that just as Christ was raised from the dead by the glory of the Father, even so we also should walk in newness of life." And so, we are buried in the watery grave of baptism. Jesus shed his blood in his death. In baptism we are buried into his death. We contact that saving blood of Christ and our sins are washed away. That's why we come out of that watery grave of baptism to walk in newness of life.

Once you have done those things, Acts 2:47 says the Lord will add you to the church.

Friends, the church of Christ still exists today just as it did in the First Century.

The way the church did in the first century. We pray, we study the Bible together. We hear preaching together. We give financially according to how God has blessed us. Christ is our only head.

Chapter Five

WHY THE WORLD IS GOING TO HELL

Some will not like this but all you have to do is watch T.V. and you will see how this world is truly going to hell. The world *is* going to hell: the fact is so obvious that it doesn't need repeating. What is not so obvious is why. In a sense it is obvious why the world is going to hell--the world does not believe Jesus is Lord. But why doesn't the world believe? That is the question, isn't it?

Paul tells us the god of this world--Satan--has blinded the eyes of the unbelievers. 2 Corinthians 4:4 "The god of this age, (world) has blinded the minds (eyes) of unbelievers, so that they cannot see the light of the gospel of the glory of Christ, who is the image of God."

That's the short answer to why the world is going to hell-- Satan has blinded the eyes of unbelievers so they can't see the gospel of Jesus Christ as Truth. And I suppose few Christians would argue with Paul about that observation. But I'd bet my last dollar there's not many Christians out there who could tell you exactly how Satan goes about blinding the eyes of the unbeliever to the glory of the God revealed in the face of Jesus Christ.

The fact that we don't have a firm fix on how Satan goes about accomplishing his goal creates great tension in the Body of Christ on earth. In our hearts, we all know that Jesus does not want anybody to perish. Regardless of how much we've fined tuned the doctrine of election, none of us are comfortable in the presence of a world going straight to hell. No matter how well we can explain why the world is going to hell and at the same time explain that God really loves the world in spite of the fact the world is going to hell, none of us are comfortable with this situation. In our hearts we still feel deep tugging that make us think all those people who don't believe in Jesus, somehow, shouldn't be going to hell. We understand clearly that Jesus gave himself to be humiliated, suffer, die, and descend into hell precisely because He wanted to prevent the world from going to hell. The fact that the world is going to hell tempts us--and the world as well--to conclude that either Jesus is not capable of accomplishing his purpose, or we are not doing what He wants us to do. Those who are in Christ Jesus are tense because we know enough about Jesus to know His Will is not the problem.

Christians have a difficult time understanding how Satan blinds the unbelievers because we don't really want to face the answer. When the Lord finally breaks through and reveals the answer to us, it shakes all us saints to our bootstraps. It shakes us because we all come face to face with the fact that judgment does begin with the Church.

The fact is Satan uses Christians to blind the unbelievers. I can hear muttering coming from the amen corner: What does he mean we don't know Satan uses Christians? That's what we've always said.

Right, but don't relax yet: remember I said *exactly* how Satan does his work. We've always had some insight into how Satan uses Christians to blind the world to the glory of Jesus. We've always known the world watches professing Christians like a hawk waiting to pounce on the slightest signs of deviation from the ethical standards defined as "Christian" so they could justify the hardness of their heart toward the life and work of Jesus

Christ. This has led to countless sermons and moved all of us to strive diligently to surrender anything that might cause anybody to stumble. But we've never quite grasped how Satan can use us to blind the eyes of the unbelievers even after we've quit fornicating and smoking and drinking and cussing and hanging around with those that do. All Satan needs is a Church full of Christians who haven't got a clue how they got saved. That's *exactly* what he needs.

Everybody knows how we got saved, you say? We got saved by believing that Jesus died for our sins and that He rose from the grave. Faith in that is how we got saved. No argument there.

Try telling the world you are saved because you believe you are saved. If believing you are saved is all there is to salvation, then the world can believe they are saved too. Jesus doesn't have to be a part of the equation if believing we are saved is all salvation requires.

You say people must believe in Jesus to be saved? So do I. That's what I say too. But I have sense enough to know that if I can't tell unbelievers why they must believe in Jesus to be saved, then I am going to make headway only with people who want to be like me, people who are willing to share my beliefs even when we don't understand exactly what we are believing.

You say we must believe in Jesus to be saved because that's what the Bible tells us to believe if we are to be saved? You say the Bible is the Word of God and that is reason enough and answer enough for anybody that is chosen to be a part of the kingdom of God? I hope so, I hope that's enough, because that is all the world is getting out of us saints today. I am writing this book, though, because I am convinced in the Lord that He wants more from us than the answers we've been giving.

I believe the Bible gives us another message to tell the world, a message that is different from the message being presented by the Church to the world today. Instead of the Bible telling us to believe in Jesus Christ because the Bible tells us to believe, I believe God wants us to believe in Jesus Christ because we understand exactly how his dying on the cross saved those who believe in Him from an eternity in hell separated from the presence of God. It is that message that I have spent the last few years receiving. I hope you'll let me tell you about it.

Chapter Six

What the Hell

I have to be bold. We have to look into some of the things being taught in our schools and steering us away from God. With the way the United States has been going down the tubes in moral downfall. Every election is leading us closer to hell in this world. Every decision made affects us. Why does everything in the United States (and the world for that matter) seem to be going to hell. Who's carrying it to hell?

Everything seems to be falling apart. If you are a Christian reading this, most of you would probably answer - There is no love left in the world. God has been removed. Satan is taking control. These are all good and correct responses; however they give no explanation as to how and why all this has come about. In addition, unless you know the how and why, one has no idea where to start to correct the problem.

I suggest that the average Christian simply doesn't know basic right from wrong. Surprised? Look at some of these Christian statements.

- Two people of the same sex should be allowed to marry or at least have a civil union if they truly love each other. Our Lord did command us to love one another.

- A 22 year-old woman is accosted by hoodlums beaten, gang raped and becomes pregnant. She opts for an abortion.

- A committed lesbian couple who have been together for 15 years wish to adopt a child. They have already helped raise the child of a family member who passed away. They have proven themselves. Let them adopt a child.
- A political candidate is running for office. He appears honest and forthright. He wants to balance the budget and promote economic prosperity and stability. He happens to be pro-choice. Your friends have decided to vote for this gentleman since his motives are pure and he is looking out for the common good.
- A student in High School science class is given the topic of earth origins as a class assignment. He approaches it from a young earth (6 thousand year) Biblical viewpoint. His research is documented with appropriate scientific references. His teacher dismisses the report on the grounds that it is not consistent with accepted geological principles. Religion is a matter of faith, and science is for the classroom.
- A child in the cafeteria blesses herself to say grace quietly before eating her lunch. A teacher notices and the girl is taken to the principal's office. The girl is told she must be tolerant of others of different faiths, and her actions could be offensive to some. Besides, she is in effect breaking the law of "separation of church and state."
- Situation Ethics and Relative Morality are University level courses, with discussions of various options in different situations, because no one can determine what is absolute moral truth. We must learn to accept other viewpoints, moral codes, religions, experiences, etc.
- You live in NYC which doesn't allow personal ownership of guns. You have been selected to serve on a jury. There was a break in to an apartment late at night. The renter heard voices. He grabbed his gun. One of the thieves entered his bedroom; he fired and killed the intruder. The renter is brought up on charges of murder and possessing an illegal weapon. There must be some punishment since the law was broken and a human being was killed.

I want to go over some of these things happening and being preached in Churches all over the world.

The Bible today has become equivalent to a buffet for Christians as a whole. Sort of pick what you like and leave what you don't. It has been proven that there are many inaccuracies, fables, old legends and myths in it. There is much metaphor and allegory, especially in Genesis, used to get certain lessons of faith across. The Bible is a book of faith and morals. It is not a history book nor a science text.

We learn about the history of the world and science in school, and faith and morals in church. In school, we are taught about how historically all space, time and matter began with the Big Bang about 15 billion years ago. Then the formation of our solar system, and earth about 4.5 billion years ago. Early rudimentary life forms began to develop about one billion plus years ago in the primitive oceans. Eventually, life moved onto the land and evolved through the amphibians, reptiles, birds, mammals, the lower primates to hominids, and then man. Upward and onward! The history of the early hunter-gatherers of 15-20 thousand years ago, and then the development of the agrarian societies. Finally, around 5 thousand or so years, language, and the written word.

Now the Bible, starting with Genesis, gives an entirely different history of the world. God created the universe and earth in six essentially 24 hour days culminating with Adam and Eve, and then Noah's Flood. All this began around six thousand years ago. Adam begat Seth who begat Enos who begat ......all the way through Abraham and eventually Jesus. This is entirely different from what is taught in school. However, schools today do teach what and how to "begat!"which is sex education.

Most people, don't think of Genesis as real history that took place in real space and time. Genesis is usually relegated to allegory, metaphor, or as a myth!

Jesus came to complete the Old Testament. Never once in all of Jesus' quotes did he ever deny any part of the Old Testament, including His quotes regarding Adam and Noah. This is absolutely crucial to understanding the creation/evolution controversy. Was Jesus a liar? Or, he obviously didn't understand evolution?! As we mumble "I believe in God.......Creator of heaven and earth."

The Bible and evolution are NOT compatible! The Bible states: Creation (Adam, animals, etc.), then Adam sins, then Noah's flood which formed the fossils (death)! On the other hand, evolution states: organisms (live and DIE) evolving toward man (call him Adam) while forming the fossil layers (DEATH) over the ages.

Upward and onward, "The secrets of evolution are death and time, death (fossils) BEFORE Adam? Reflect on this heresy!

Man, by his sin nature (remember Adam & the forbidden fruit), doesn't really like being answerable to anyone. Of course if you are a faithful evolutionist, then by definition there is no such thing as "sin." You decide right and wrong. You evolved from that and are answerable to no one. Think back when you were a teenager. Oh yeah, the original "Rebel Without a Cause." This is why are world looks to the world to save itself. We only need to look to God to save this world.

Either the God of the Bible created all the physical laws and entities that the universe abides by or He didn't – period. All sciences are based on facts. The facts for a creationist and evolutionist are the same facts. It's the Interpretation of those facts that is different, and hence one's world view (Creation/God-based or evolution/blind chance-based) is subsequently formed depending on which set of facts you adhere to. That is why we are briefly reviewing the various scientific fields. The modern worldview of the sciences interprets the facts to favor evolution. My goal is to present to you a creationist interpretation of those SAME facts.

If everything in this universe is here by blind random chance, then you are answerable to no one but yourself; there is no absolute right and wrong. BUT, if evolution is just a hoax and the evidence weighs against it, then ALL the science should also support a creationist position and repudiate an evolutionary based one. Reject the Ten Commandments then at your own peril. Wow what crazy talk. We as a Church are sitting in this world quiet with no voice.

All the scientific evidence should conclude with creation over evolution. If even one of the scholarships supports fully and unequivocally evolution, then there can be no omnipotent, omniscience God of the Bible. Point is, if the God of the Bible is the great "I Am", this should be reflected in EVERY scientific discipline, and the weight of evidence should be overwhelming. Hang with me – it is!

Remember if evolution is true, when you die you go back to nothing but worm food. You don't have to worry about a heaven or hell, reward or retribution. That is what makes evolution so attractive. This is all there is, get the most you can, while you can, anyway you can. "Do unto others BEFORE they do unto you", the atheistic evolutionary perverted Golden rule.

This is exactly why you can have a Roman Catholic priest be a pedophile. There is no way he can believe in God. He can state on the pulpit that he does, but he doesn't. I respect avowed atheists more, at least they are honest as to their belief in God – they don't! Standing in a garage saying you are car doesn't make you a car, any more than standing in the pulpit in a church saying you are a preacher. A man of God involved in pederasty has to believe in evolution to a large degree. If he truly believed in the God of all Creation and that He has every hair on our heads counted, aware of the sparrow that falls, given every star a name – there is NO way he could perform such vile acts. And remember this is a minister that has taken vows. Do we really need then to explain the acts (and legislation) of various seedy congressmen, senators, international bankers, Supreme court justices, the Federal Reserve and your next door neighbor or co-worker as to why they act the way they do against God and His laws?

How about the ACLU and its relentless attack on Christians and Christmas? Nativity scenes are a favorite appetizer for them. If evolution is true, then these atheists are correct in asking for the removal of anything related to religion or God – since He really doesn't exist. (as they believe) Kind of like Santa Claus, the Easter Bunny and the Tooth Fairy. They really are all in the same category of nonsensical characters. Sorry, I just can't help myself. The universe created itself from nothing (blind random chance). "In the beginning hydrogen…."

Definition of sin is rebellion against God. If the entire Cosmos and all it contains are here by blind random chance, obviously there can't BE a God, i.e. therefore no sin. Sin is exclusively a religious concept. How can you accuse anyone of sinning if not using a religious (Christian) context to do so? Under evolution how can you possibly judge anyone of a sin? Therefore anything is allowed – except Christianity (which judges peoples actions based on a religious/Creationist context.) And death has been around for "millions of years", UNLESS there really was an Adam and Eve (6000 years) who did commit the first sin (disobeying God by eating the forbidden fruit) and the punishment was death. In old Hebrew, "die" translates to "In dying you will die", since Adam and Eve didn't die immediately after God's judgment on them. That is why you see "tolerance" pushed into every aspect of society. Anything goes, anything is permitted – except judgmental Christianity of course. We use phrases such as a "post modern society" and "no longer a Christian nation", but we don't know why. We are an evolution, or should I say "evolution" based culture now. Easily 90% of the problems we read or see on the news are directly or indirectly evolution related. Even the lame stream media themselves are lying to us. I'm sorry. I apologize. Since we are an evolution based society, how can there be such a thing as a "lie"? If evolution is true, lies are only abstract concepts.

This is clear heresy for a Christian to hold to the evolutionary position of "millions of years," which by definition MUST represent millions of years of death before Adam evolved. Actually Adam was created (out of nothing) by Almighty God. The female of the species, Eve, would have had to evolve at the same time and location as the male.

Why is the world going to hell? One reason is we have received hell's teaching more than God's teacheing.

Chapter Seven

Going to Hell

If we as a Church leave our heads in the clouds, we will not see the world as it really is. One might wonder how the people of "the world" are able to stay blind in this very prophetic time in history. Personally, I was one of those people living in blissful ignorance, not so long ago. I was one of those Christians who weren't really a Christian in my early years, but was told to like that I was, so I didn't question it. I didn't look inside to see if I was a Christian. I didn't question my standing with God. I just lived my life without much thought of the eternity. From what I knew, I was saved because I believed in Jesus. I had my ticket into heaven and no one could snatch me out of His hand from what I understood. Yet, I never read the Bible, I rarely went to church most of my life, and I didn't worry about it either. I didn't feel guilty about my sin because hey it was paid for by Jesus and was not going to be remembered by God, so who was I to dwell on it?

We have to remember that people are blind, and "we" have the ointment that can cure them. Yet, it seems that even in the church people are passing the buck to someone else to do the dirty work of spreading the Gospel. We just want to reap the benefits of being a Christian without doing the work of a follower. True Christian's know without a doubt that most churches these days are not giving the full Gospel, so they know that people who are looking to find God in church are still blind after they leave their hip, concert-like, coffee selling churches. Do these blind parishioners know they are blind or do they walk out feeling like they got something spiritual? I can tell you that I was a volunteer in my seeker sensitive church for years and never once questioned my standing with God. I loved going to that church and never thought that it was a watered down message. In fact,

I was sure that my sins were forgiven and didn't even question my habitual sin. In truth, Christians can go out drinking with friends and have no feelings of guilt, for we are not expected to be perfect. Once I learned the truth by simply picking up my Bible and reading it, my church actually seemed irritated by my desire to make sure people were told the whole truth. I think churches that are more concerned about keeping people of the world in a comfortable state of ignorance are more dangerous than anything the world is lying to them about. We can't sneak sinners into heaven's gate without them experiencing the change of heart that only the true unfiltered gospel can do. The world is wide open with what it offers...sin, sin and more sin. When a church tells you "just repeat this prayer after me and you are saved" is a much more evil lie.

People stay blind because that is the state of mind they are living in. We can't point our judgmental fingers at blind people doing what blind people do. We must care about them enough to break out of our own little comfortable worlds and tell them the truth. We must risk our reputations among the blind and live with the labels they may attach to us...because we love them more than ourselves. Christ who lives in us loves them, so we love them. True Christians are reading the signs of the times and they know their Lord draws near, yet they are keeping quiet? Why? False Christians do not know they are false. False Christian are no safer than believers of other faiths. They may be more blind than the rest because they "think" they know the truth. This world is passing away before our eyes, the Lord gave us instructions to preach the word to all...what are we waiting for? If you are a true Christian, you have your instructions. God didn't save you just so you could sit on your hands and do nothing to further His kingdom. If you believe that, then you just might be one of those false Christians who don't know it. If you don't know how to spread the word, there are many programs that teach you how...but you must seek them out to find them. Search your heart to see if you are really in the faith. If you are afraid to search because you might find that you are not truly a Christian, it is better to find out now rather than on Judgment Day. Time is running out.

Christ did His job, what are you doing for Him? For all those out there "doing" a lot for Christ, make sure you're heart and intentions are in the right place. I say that because so many religions out there create lots of "good" people who do "good" things, but they are still lost. Doing good for Christ doesn't make you a Christian, if you are just doing it to get into heaven. Believing in Christ as your only way into heaven is the only thing that gets you there. Doing good after that fact is not because we are good, but because He is good. He does His good through His flock. He gets the credit, not you. We spread the word to the world because He died for those lost people, and He loves them and He is using us to get to them. Are you doing His will by allowing Him to use you? Or are you too busy? Or not a good speaker? Or too shy? Or some other reason that you tell yourself is an acceptable excuse? There is no more time for excuses. It is time to speak up for Christ and give the whole truth to this lost and dying world. It isn't someone else's job. It's yours and mine and every single Christian you know. Right across the street from you or next door or someone in your family is someone who is heading in the direction of hell. Are they going to hell? You don't need to go to another country mission field. Pray for God to give you boldness to speak His word and He will because that is His will. That prayer will be answered, so get ready to work for Christ. We all know that we could all do better, me included, so let's do it today! I pray that God will not allow you to sink back into your comfortable complacency, but will give you the love it takes to do His work.

Chapter Eight

The Dead Church

How does a Church become a form of Godliness but denying the power there of. How does a Church become dead. We will look into some of this in this Chapter and I hope resurrection life comes upon us all not to be a dead Church.

Sardis write,

These things says He who has the seven Spirits of God and the seven stars: "I know your works, that you have a name that you are alive, but you are dead. ²Be watchful, and strengthen the things which remain, that are ready to die, for I have not found your works perfect before God. ³Remember therefore how you have received and heard; hold fast and repent. Therefore if you will not watch, I will come upon you as a thief, and you will not know what hour I will come upon you. ⁴You have a few names even in Sardis who have not defiled their garments; and they shall walk with Me in white, for they are worthy. ⁵He who overcomes shall be clothed in white garments, and I will not blot out his name from the Book of Life; but I will confess his name before My Father and before His angels. ⁶"He who has an ear, let him hear what the Spirit says to the churches."

Here are some signs to an unhealthy Church,

1) Leadership has no clear vision.

2) Leadership can never be challenged.

3) You are comfortable but never challenged.

4) Members are content with being pew warmers.

5) Outreach is never planned or preached.

All of these are true, but there is so much more.

6). Prayer, if offered at all, is a formality, an afterthought, a burden.

There is no more accurate indicator of a Christian's spirituality or a church's health than the strength of our prayer life.

7) Giving stems from duty and is never a joy.

"God loves a hilarious giver," we're told in II Corinthians 9:7.

When David was receiving the offering to build the original temple, he was so impressed by the joyful spirit of the givers. Scripture says, "Then the people rejoiced for they had offered willingly, because with a loyal heart they had offered willingly to the Lord, and King David also rejoiced greatly" (I Chronicles 29:9).

....not grudgingly or of necessity, for God loves a cheerful giver. (II Corinthians 9:7)

8) Laughter is rare, and when present at all, forced and quickly stifled.

Someone asked a friend of mine, "Do you think Jesus ever laughed? The Bible doesn't say He did." My buddy's answer is as good as it gets: "I don't know whether he laughed or not. But He sure fixed me up so I could!"

We are "fixed up to laugh," Christian. Joy is the very atmosphere of the Throne room of Heaven (Psalms 16:11) and laughter is nothing but audible joy.

The preacher who thinks he has to tell jokes to elicit laughter from his people is missing the point. The difference in that kind of provoked joy and the natural joy that arises from the hearts of happy worshipers is the difference in night and day.

9) When church ends, everyone scatters.

I understand that when the meeting is over but let me tell you something; when our full team of ministry hangs around after a service there is greater unity. Church members should love each other like they cannot wait to get together. "By this all men will know you are my disciples," our Lord said, "that you love one another" (John 13:34-35).

10) When a leader calls for volunteers, he gets few responses.

Leaders can lead, but if no one is following, they're only taking a walk. It takes both strong leaders of courage and vision, commitment and strength, and volunteers from among the Lord's people who will step up to go the second mile, do a little more than previously, exert themselves for the success of the work.

The congregation that is forced to rely on the same few overworked volunteers is on life-support.

11) When conflict arises, leaders ignore it, push the panic button, or jump ship.

A sick church will go to one extreme or the other: it will panic at any conflict, thinking this will be the final death-stroke, or it will be constantly beset by conflict, like a sickly body experiencing one illness after another.

Stand in awe at the healthy way the Jerusalem church leaders dealt with the conflict of Acts 6 that had erupted. Both leaders and members reacted so quickly and faithfully that outsiders were impressed. *Then the Word of God spread, and the number* of disciples multiplied greatly in Jerusalem, and a great many of the priests were obedient to the faith.*

A healthy church will often have growing pains, will regularly be attacked by the enemy, and will always have to be ready to deal with problems from inside and out. (see Acts 20:29-30)

12) Even the leaders have a poor understanding of Scripture.

A working knowledge of God's Word is like the foundation of a house; it may not be the first thing you notice, but everything about the dwelling will be influenced by that strong foundation.

13) Jesus and the Holy Spirit is rarely mentioned. It's all about "God."

Those who know the Word cannot get around the prominence Jesus Christ receives throughout. Scripture says, "In Him dwells all the fullness of the Godhead bodily" (Colossians 2:9). And, "He is the visible image of the invisible God" (Colossians 1:15).

"Jesus Christ is everything God has to say about Himself." Jesus said, "He who has seen me has seen the Father" (John 14:9), and "When the Holy Spirit comes... He will testify of Me" (John 15:26).

I confess to being amazed sometimes at the way Christians speak of serving God, living for God, etc., while leaving Jesus out of it. The early believers were persecuted, not for preaching about God, but speaking of Jesus. (Acts 4:18) Had they been silent about Jesus, there would have been no persecution.

14) No one hears about salvation, no one gets saved, the baptism is dry.

This is not to say that all churches taking in large numbers of new members and baptizing many hundreds are automatically proven healthy. Unfortunately, one can use gimmicks to get people to join a church and manipulate them to be baptized. I say to our shame that many churches resort to this rather than trod the hard road of building a healthy church. A large Church may contain few saved Christians.

I chose and appointed you that you should go and bear fruit, and that your fruit should remain....(John 15:16).

15) Neither the members nor the leaders are willing to pay the price to make the church healthy.

Going from death-bed to health requires sacrifice, commitment, work, and often pain. It will require the patient to make wholesale changes, to submit to the oversight of medical professionals who know more than the diseased patient and know what to prescribe. It will require a willingness to die to self.

That's why a truly sick-unto-death church would rather die than live. In order to be healthy, they would have to stop their self-destructive ways, retire some unhealthy leaders, and become a kind of church they have not been in years, if ever.

Right at this moment, I can take you to a-dozen churches that are dying and which have rejected the good counsel of friends who told them what it would take to be well. It was for good reason our Lord asked the man at the pool of Bethesda, "Do you want to be well?" (John 5:6). Not everyone does.

The good news, however, is that I know an equal number of small formerly-dying churches which have welcomed in new outside leadership and put themselves completely in their hands. These specialists are making wholesale changes--beginning with renaming the church altogether--and none of this is taking place without pain.

It's good for all of us, members and leaders alike, to remind ourselves every day of our lives of three things:

This is the Lord's church. He died for it, I didn't. (Matthew 16:18)

The only question is "What does He want done with His church?" (Acts 9:6)

Whatever I do for the church, good or bad, Jesus takes personally. (Acts 9:3,5; Matthew 25:40,45).

Spiritually Dead

For much of the past three decades, denominational officials have been promoting seminars and programs aimed at revitalizing the church. I know because I have been the speaker or consultant to many of these groups. For many of these leaders, their goal was to breathe new life into churches experiencing declining memberships and lack of commitment. Yet after years of trying to revitalize these churches, the vast majority of them are still declining. What gives?

Reformation, renewal, and revitalization assume some pre-existing foundation of faith from which to raise up a new church. But what if that assumption isn't correct? What if the assumption is part of our problem? What if being a member of a church for 40 years doesn't automatically guarantee any spiritual depth? What if holding every office in the church doesn't automatically mean someone is a disciple of Jesus Christ? Do we dare look deep enough into our souls to find answers to these questions?

I have concluded that most leaders are spiritually dead and their institutions have ceased being the church. They have the form but not the substance of what it means to be the church.

Let me define what I mean by spiritually dead churches. If your church spends most of its energy on itself and its members, it's spiritually dead.

Such churches are living corpses. They are physically alive; some may even be growing; but they are spiritually dead to the mission of the New Testament church-to make disciples of Jesus Christ. They've turned inward and exist solely for themselves.

They look for ways to serve themselves, and the kingdom be damned.

They're like baby birds sitting in the nest with their mouths open waiting for momma bird (pastor) to feed them with no concept that Jesus intends them to feed others. Oh, they might collect money to send away to some distant mission field, but they're all thumbs when it comes to sharing the good news with their neighbor or community. What growth they might experience is not of their doing-it just happens because of the population growth around them.

Let's look at some keys to what makes a Church spiritually dead.

1. Have lost their sense of mission to those who have not heard about Jesus Christ and do not pant after the Great Commission;

2. Exist primarily to provide fellowship for the "members of the club;"

3. Expect their pastors to focus primarily on ministering to the members' personal spiritual needs;

4. Design ministry to meet the needs of their members;

5. Have no idea about the needs of the "stranger outside the gates;"

6. Are focused more on the past than the future;

7. And watch the bottom line of the financial statement more than the number of confessions of faith.

Bringing life back

The starting point for unfreezing a stuck organizational system is the development of a solid community of faith that includes spiritual leaders, the absence of major conflict, trust, and a desire to connect with the unchurched world.

True spiritual maturity is approached when people turn their attention to those outside the church and seek ways to spread the good news rather than exercise their entitlements as members. Unfortunately, too many pastors assume their church has spiritual leaders and skip right over this starting point. It has become apparent to me that most church leaders do not understand that the decline of their church is due to the lack of spiritual depth on the part of their leadership.

So, now, I want to go deeper on the spiritual issue. It's not just that our churches are stuck; they are spiritually bankrupt!

I know. These churches are filled mostly with good Christian people, but there's no discernable spiritual power, just good Christian people-and we all know what Jesus said about being good. (Mark 10:18)

So it's obvious. Isn't it? The only solution for spiritually dead congregations is resurrection. You can't revitalize something that is dead. They must be brought to life again! And that is resurrection.

Revival can be a waste of time. God has broken revival's out in some place but the Cities have missed it. You can't breathe life into a corpse. Only God can do that, and that is resurrection.

Resurrecting a church

My experience has taught me the resurrection of a church happens in three stages. It begins with a new pastor. Either the pastor experiences a personal resurrection or the church actually gets a new pastor. Next is the resurrection of the leaders of the church either by transformation or replacement. Finally, the church itself is resurrected and turned around through some tactical change. Then, if resurrection happens, our behavior changes:

1. The church turns outward in its focus.

2. Jesus, not the institution, will become the object of our affection.

3. The Great Commission will become our mandate, and we will measure everything we do by how many new converts we make rather than whether we have a black bottom line.

4. Membership in the Kingdom will replace membership in the church.

5. Pastors will cease being chaplains of pastoral care and will become modern-day apostles of Jesus Christ.

6. And those who try to control the church with an iron fist or intimidate the church at every turn of the road will be shown the door.

    The primary reason society is shunning the institutional church is because for the most part it is spiritually dead. Spiritually alive churches, no matter what their form or where they are planted, always grow. That is the nature of the beast. That is the kind of church God honors. That is what the church was put on earth to do-spread the good news. When a church faithfully does that, it grows. Period."

About the Author

Bill Vincent is an Apostle and Author with Revival Waves of Glory Ministries in Litchfield, IL. Bill and his wife Tabitha work closely in every day ministry duties. Bill and Tabitha lead a team providing Apostolic over sight in all aspects of ministry, including service, personal ministry and Godly character.

Bill is a believer in Jesus Christ in the fullness of power with signs and wonders. Bill has an accurate prophetic gift, a powerful revelatory preaching anointing with miracles signs and wonders following.

Bill Vincent is no stranger to understanding the power of God, having spent over twenty years as a Minister with a strong prophetic anointing, which taught him the importance of deliverance by the power of God. Bill has more than thirty prophetic books available all over the world. Prior to starting his ministry, Revival Waves of Glory he spent the last few years as a Pastor of a Church and a traveling prophetic ministry.

Bill Vincent helps the Body of Christ to get closer to God while overcoming the enemy. Bill offers a wide range of writings and teachings from deliverance, to the presence of God and Apostolic cutting edge Church structure. Drawing on the power of the Holy Spirit through years of experience in Revival, Spiritual Sensitivity and deliverance ministry, Bill now focuses mainly on pursuing the Presence of God and breaking the power of the devil off of people's lives.

His book Defeating the Demonic Realm was published in 2011 and has since helped many people to overcome the spirits and curses of satan. Since then Bill's books have flooded the market with his writings released just like he prophesies the Word of the Lord.

Bill Vincent is a unique man of God whom has discovered; powerful ways to pursue God's presence, releasing revelations of the demonic realm and prophetic anointing through everything he does. Bill is always moving forward at a rapid pace and there is sure to be much more released by him in upcoming years.

Recommended Books

By Bill Vincent

Overcoming Obstacles

Glory: Pursuing God's Presence

Defeating the Demonic Realm

Increasing Your Prophetic Gift

Increasing Your Anointing

Keys to Receiving Your Miracle

The Supernatural Realm

Waves of Revival

Increase of Revelation and Restoration

The Resurrection Power of God

Discerning Your Call of God

Apostolic Breakthrough

Glory: Increasing God's Presence

Love is Waiting – Don't Let Love Pass You By

The Healing Power of God

Glory: Expanding God's Presence

Receiving Personal Prophecy

Signs and Wonders

Signs and Wonders Revelations

Children Stories

Rapture Revelations

The Secret Place of God's Power

Building a Prototype Church

Breakthrough of Spiritual Strongholds

Glory: Revival Presence of God

The Watchman of the Lord

Overcoming the Power of Lust

Glory: Kingdom Presence of God

Children Stories 10 Book Series

Faith Bible Adventures

Transitioning Into a Prototype Church

The Stronghold of Jezebel

Healing After Divorce

A Closer Relationship With God

Cover Up and Save Yourself

The Watchman of the Lord 2

Desperate for God's Presence

The War for Spiritual Battles

Spiritual Leadership

By Bill Vincent, Paula Loveless, Joseph Basurto, Jackie Money and more

Experience God's Love

By Bishop Gregory Leachman

God's Greatest Challenge:

Man & His Ungodly Ways

Conforming to the Mind of Christ

A Deeper Conforming to the Mind of Christ

By Richard Money

My Life in a Salami Factory

Journey of Faith (EPOS Edition)

By Kevin Cann

Who Is Your Source

By Mark Krenning

More of Him, Less of Me

By Jeff Beacham

In the Shadow of Eternity

By Bill Easter

Journey Into the Apostolic

By Don Babin

Outreach

Connect With Jesus

By Eddie Smith

And

Michael L. Hennen

Strategic Prayer

By Janet Basurto

Never Forsaken

By Joseph Basurto

One Accord Love

By Wallace Henley

Spillover: War In Heaven

To Order:

Email:

rwgcontact@yahoo.com

Web Site:

www.revivalwavesofgloryministries.com

Mail Order:

Revival Waves of Glory

PO Box 596

Litchfield, IL 62056

Shipping $5.00

Prices do not include shipping and are subject to change. If you mail an order and pay by check, make check out to Revival Waves of Glory.

Most books are in multiple formats such as Hardcover, Soft-Cover, Ebook (such as Kindle & Nook), and Audio Books.

www.ingramcontent.com/pod-product-compliance
Lightning Source LLC
Chambersburg PA
CBHW072113290426
44110CB00014B/1900